THE SEDONA VORTEX EXPERIENCE

CONTENTS:

Introduction	
What is a Vortex?	3
Sedona - My Vortex	4
The Call of the Canyon	5
The Invisible as Real	5
Sensing the Invisible	6
Nature's Dynamic Healing Energy	6
Sound	7
Temperature	7
Color	8
The Form and the Formless	9
The Breath of Oneness	9
Sedona Power Points - Map	10 - 11
Centering and Grounding	12
Centering in the Hara	12
Grounding	12
Intregration	13
The Spirals as a Universal Vortex	14
The Spiraling Dance of Life	14
Egg Beater	15
Hula Hoop	15
Be Like a Bird in Flight	16
Extend Into the Vast Magnificence of Your Being	16
Vortex Affirmations	17
Images From the Past	18
Tuning Into the Deja Vu	18
Taking the Magic Home	19
Anchoring the Experience	19
Become a Vortex of Healing Energy for the Earth	20
Major Power Points for the Sedona Vortex Experience	21

INTRODUCTION

We are in the midst of a tremendous evolutionary process. Advanced energy systems, coming in with the New Age, are forcing us to find new flexibilities. We must release old forms, embody the new energies, and transform our entire physical existence on this planet.

Many people feel that they should be able to sit down, quiet their mind, meditate, and then be at peace. Even advanced meditators are not always finding Inner Peace an easy task. People who are striving for harmonic convergence find that they are instead, experiencing "caccaphonic divergence." Why?

This new Aquarian Age is a time of pouring spirit into the earth. It is a time to fully embody our Divinity, a time of Heaven on Earth. And so, centering, aligning, and grounding these new energies is of utmost importance. Not only is meditating upon "The Light" important, but now being the embodiment of LIGHT is required. There can be no enlightened state until the entire body, consciousness, and being are cleared, lightened, and ready to receive and embody the energies of enlightenment.

Early in this century, Sri Aurobindo and The Mother began mapping this new territory for us. They wrote about the supramental energies and the supramental mind that would some day awaken. They opened up new levels of consciousness for us - levels that approach the transformation of DNA and the total release of death from our nature.

My teachers on the physical plane - Reg Newbon of the Charter For World Light, and Emily Conrad D'Aoud, innovator of Continuum Dance Meditation, as well as other gifted teachers - are leading many to a transformed state of consciousness. From form to formlessness, each in his or her own particular modality, is assisting us in preparing our minds and bodies for the bliss and ecstasy of this transformed state. "A state of bliss and ecstasy," said Sri Aurobindo, "that in our wildest imagination we can't even conceive of."

These deeper, formless states of consciousness cannot be taught, but we can begin to open ourselves up to receive new energy, bliss, and ecstasy by aligning with the natural flows of movement in the universe., These universal processes form the basic exercises in this booklet. By practicing The Sedona Vortex Experience wherever we go, we may emerge within this life's incarnation to a totally new state of being - like the first fish who wriggled out of the water and crawled onto land.

Besides practicing the exercises in this booklet and embodying the energies of The Sedona Vortex Experience, I strongly urge you to find a teacher who can assist you in opening up these new territories of consciousness. As we learn to ride the waves of quantum change in flexibility, love and joy, we will find ourselves, like the proverbial butterfly, awakened from a deep sleep and transformed into a lighter, brighter being.

Gayle Johansen
Sedona, Arizona
August 11, 1987

WHAT IS A VORTEX?

The word vortex comes from the Latin word "vertere" which means "to turn or whirl." The dictionary defines the word "vortex" as a form of fluid motion in which particles travel in a circular path around an axis. Water going down a drain forms a whirlpool or fluid vortex. Larger whirlpools are seen in the ocean. There, a whirling mass of water forms a vacuum and draws anything in its path into the center of the whirlpool.

Air is another type of fluid motion that can create a vortex. We have all seen pictures of - if not experienced - the powerful eddies of air that create whirlwinds and tornadoes. A vortex can form behind any blunt object that has some fluid flowing over it. As examples, the wind blowing around a house or water flowing around a boulder, form vortices.

From these examples - whirlpool, whirlwind, tornado - we see that a vortex has a definite shape, form, pattern, power, energy, and force. A vortex is often seen as a spiraling cone or funnel shape of awesome energy.

The dictionary also says that "any activity, situation or state of affairs that resembles a whirl or eddy in its rushing, absorbing effect, irresistible and catastrophic power, etc." is also defined as a vortex.

SEDONA - MY VORTEX

"I sat down on a vortex and haven't been the same since," is a humorous statement often voiced by many Sedonans. Is Sedona a vortex of powerful energy? Does Sedona have some absorbing, irresistible, and at times catastrophic power? Ask any resident. The stories are as many and as varied as the people who live here.

"I was driving across country, tired of the freeways and thought I'd take a short, scenic, side trip. I got off I-17, took 179 toward Sedona. When I saw Bell Rock I burst into tears. I pulled off the road, walked to the base of that great monolith, fell down, hugged the rocks, and kissed the earth. I knew I was home!"

"Everything kept coming up Sedona," another true story begins. "I'd never been to Sedona, but I kept hearing about it from family, friends, strangers, on the radio, and on T.V. Something kept ringing a bell inside me every time I heard the word Sedona. One day I picked up a magazine at the grocery check out counter, opened it, and there was an article on 'Sedona.' That's it, I thought. I've got to check that place out...that was ten years ago. I think that Sedona is actually checking me out."

"I had been unhappy to the point of illness for some time. I started seeing my Baptist minister for counseling. We would always start the session with a prayer and ask the Holy Spirit for guidance and healing. After about five sessions I began feeling that my problems and illness were caused by the stress of the big city. 'I think I need to move to the country,' I said one day. My minister closed his eyes in prayer and then burst out with: 'Yes, and Spirit is telling me where.' 'Tell me,' I begged. 'No, that's for you to find out.'
The next day in the midst of smog, honking, and bumper to bumper traffic on the L.A. freeway, I felt a deep inner peace. I looked up at the car in front of me and saw a 'Sedona' bumper-sticker. I had an incredible rush of energy and tears welled up in my eyes.
'Sedona!' I said to my minister, that Sunday at church.
'You're very intuitive.' he smiled back."

Each person that has come to this land has seen the canyon open into a lush green valley along the creek bed. We have watched the sculpted Red Rocks leap up before us in almost mystical form. We have witnessed the naked edges of sandstone and basalt bend and stand silhouetted against the changing skies. And each of us has felt the power, mystery, and magic of this land called Sedona.

THE CALL OF THE CANYON

People of all ages and walks of life hear the call of the canyon and are drawn to Sedona by the magic that is here. Artists see the magic as beauty. Retired folks experience the magic as clean air, country living, good health - qualities of the good life. Spiritually-oriented people are drawn to Sedona like moths to a flame, without even knowing why they came. Many people have had the experience of being "called" to Sedona without any awareness of the power, mystery, and magic that is here.

Recently Dick Sutphen and Page Bryant have written about Sedona as one of the major power points on the planet. Planet Earth is a living, changing, evolving being, that has places of power on it, much like we have acupressure points on our bodies. The power points or vorticies on the planet are places where energy can be seen, felt, and experienced. Unusual phenomena often occur at these places.

THE INVISIBLE AS REAL

In our materialistic culture, if we cannot see a thing with our physical eyes, we tend to think it doesn't exist. Yet we can see that energy and matter embody both the dense structures of New York skyscrapers as well as the lighter structures of fog and mist.

A pot of homemade soup brewing in the kitchen can definitely be perceived by someone in another part of the house. But what of things that the physical senses cannot pick up - energies that reach beyond our five physical senses? These energies are real, too. We need to develop new ways of seeing, smelling, touching, sensing, etc. in order to experience not only the Sedona Vortex energies, but the energies of our own vast, multi-dimensional beingness as well.

SENSING THE INVISIBLE

This is a fun, basic, energy-sensing exercise that will help you feel similarities and differences in the energies of Sedona Vortex areas.

Rub the palms of your hands briskly together for 10 -15 seconds. Then, place your palms facing each other, with about an inch between them. Feel the sensation. Move your hands farther apart, then closer together as though they are held together by a rubber band. Feel the energy. When the feeling decreases, stimulate your palms again.

With a partner, hold your palms a few inches apart from each other and imagine that you have taffy between your hands. See how far you can extend the feeling without breaking the sense of connection.

Cup your hands around a flower, or slightly out from the trunk of a tree. Feel and sense the plant's auric energy field. Put your palms down toward the earth and feel the energy emanating upward.

Now you can tune into the energies of the land by holding your hands up and feeling the energies coming toward you.

Feel the energies start to rise.

NATURE'S DYNAMIC HEALING ENERGY

All of nature is available to us to help us clear, heal, and release old traumas, emotional scars, and habituated thought patterns. The key is being receptive to Nature's dynamic healing energy. The following series of exercises will assist you in opening up to the healing energies in Nature.

After centering and grounding, move into a posture of receiving. Find a comfortable place, sit down, place your hands palms up on your lap, and inhale deeply. Receive Nature's gift of fresh, healing air. Relax your shoulders, slowly shake or spiral out any held tension. Roll your head and neck from side to side. Then focus on one of the following areas: Sound, Temperature, or Color.

SOUND Place the palms of your hands over your ears while breathing deeply. Allow the soft movement of your breath to rise up through your neck into your head and brain. Then remove your hands and begin to focus on the sounds that you hear. Let your consciousness extend into each different sound. Then become one with all the sounds. Feel the waves of sound energy, starting at your outer ears, flowing into your inner ears. Let the waves of energy blend into one pulsating movement.

Accept the sounds of Nature - the sounds outside of yourself - as background music for your own inner sound of silence. Breathe into that inner core of silence. Allow the sounds and the silence to become a spiraling vortex of energy that propels you into your Divinity.

Listen to the musical sound of the creek as the water goes bellowing, murmuring and tinkling over the rocks. Allow the sound to wash through your body and mind. Let the soft, soothing sound flow through your consciousness, carrying away any debris left there by emotional storms. You can use the sounds of the birds and/or the bees in a similar manner as the above exercises. You can also "pretend" that you are the water, the birds, bees, or the sound-maker and then allow that experience to carry you into an inseparable oneness with all of Nature's dynamic healing energy.

TEMPERATURE Sitting or lying in a comfortable place, begin to feel the warmth of the sun on your body. Let the warmth of the sun radiate deep into your bones - into your very core. Allow the warm feeling to spread out over your entire body. Let the warmth and the light from the sun fill every cell, tissue and muscle of your body. Imagine yourself in the heart of the sun. Imagine the sun radiating in your heart center. Breathe deeply and experience your magnificence.

Feel the cool breeze on your skin. Notice its gentle caress. Let its formlessness dance across your physical form. Allow your consciousness to join the dancing breeze. Breathe with the breeze. Let yourself expand. Feel more space both within your physical form and within the formlessness of your conscious awareness. Notice the breeze dancing in the trees. Notice a similar dancing movement somewhere in your body. Let yourself feel kissed, caressed, and loved by the breeze. Let the feeling of love fill your body and being. Then, get up and dance!

Note: All attunement exercises in this booklet are in bold type.

COLOR   To relax your eyes, cover them with the palms of your hands. Inhale deeply and imagine the fresh air going to your eyes and soothing them. After a time, open your eyes. Let them softly "float" around the area - noticing all the colors in Nature. Let your eyes pick one color at a time and begin to "bring" it in.

THE RED ROCKS: Red stimulates. Breathe in the red color of the rocks. Breathe the color in through your eyes and then through your very body. Slowly drink in the color of the Red Rocks. Use the red energy to stimulate your organs and nervous system into releasing the old energy patterns that are no longer appropriate in the New Age. Allow the exhale to release and spiral away these energies. Continue breathing in the color of the Red Rocks and exhaling stagnant energies until you feel complete.

GREEN FOLIAGE: The greens in nature soothe and balance the emotional body. Pick <u>one</u> green color. (The human eye can distinguish over 300,000 shades of green!) Slowly breathe in the specific green foliage color of your choice.

Breathe the green color into your eyes and then into and through your entire body. Allow it to penetrate every cell, fiber, and tissue of your body. Allow the healing green color to soothe and balance any area of your body that seems out of alignment. Drink in the green color through your breath and through your inner and outer vision until you feel completely soothed, balanced, and healed. You may need to repeat this exercise several times for each area of emotional imbalance until all tension is displaced.

A thousand shades of foliage green

SKY BLUE : Blue is another healing color. Look up at the beautiful blue sky. (You may want to lie on your back for this exercise.) Drink in the healing, peaceful blue color of the sky. Breathe into the areas of your body, mind, or life that seem to need this kind of healing energy. Continue breathing and drinking in the sky blue color until the area of specific need is healed, whole, and complete.

WHITE CLOUDS: White represents purity, clarity, and spirit-uality. White actually contains all colors, while black is the absence of color. Breathe and drink in the color of white. Let it permeate your entire consciousness. Use any of the ideas from the above colors to complete this exercise for yourself.

Use any other colors in Nature that you are drawn to - the color of the creek water, the color of a ripe blackberry, the color of a wildflower.

THE FORM AND THE FORMLESS

The atmosphere, ethers, and air that we breathe are filled with the energies of life. Scientists call this vast fluid of cosmic soup "interplanetary plasma". The formless energies of this interplanetary plasma are called into form, action, and being every day, moment-to-moment by our very breath.

Breath is life, energy, movement. Through our breath, we are linked to every other living thing on the planet. Our breath is automatic; yet, it is the only unconscious function over which we can take immediate, conscious control. Thus, our breath serves as a bridge, carrying us from unconscious robot-like existence to beings of conscious awareness and then into masters of super-conscious abilities.

With deep, conscious inhalations we can begin to feel our held energies loosen, lift, and expand. As we breathe deeply, our energies become like a colorful bouquet of balloons - graceful, flexible and joyfully moving in the free flow of life and energy around them, all the while anchored to their source. Throughout times, cultures, and religions, breath has been linked to spirit and spiritual realms. We can re-establish this link to spirit, source, and oneness with the following exercise:

THE BREATH OF ONENESS This is a wondrous breath that depolarizes the body, gives us an immediate state of relaxation and well-being, and produces a profound state of Oneness. Take the time to master it now. Let the breath, through your nose, become full, deep and slow. Imagine that you are holding a hardboiled egg in your mouth. The lips are closed, teeth are apart, the back of the tongue is depressed while the front is cradled inside the bottom gums. On the exhale there is a sound of air being released. The exhale is the key here. Pretend you are clearing the back of your nose and throat and you will have the sound, and the exhale needed for this breath. Then, soften the sound, breath, and exhale movement. Practice this until you feel a deep, profound state of relaxation, peace, and Oneness. Then, imagine that you are exhaling down your throat, down your spine, down your legs, and into the Earth.

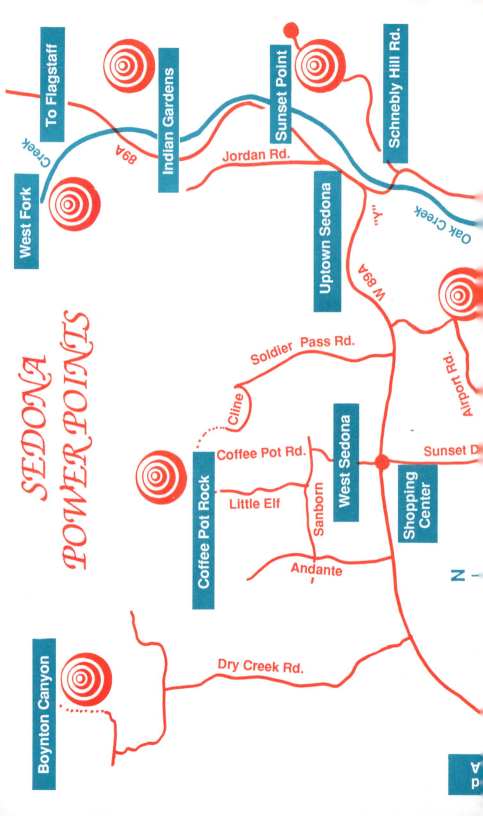

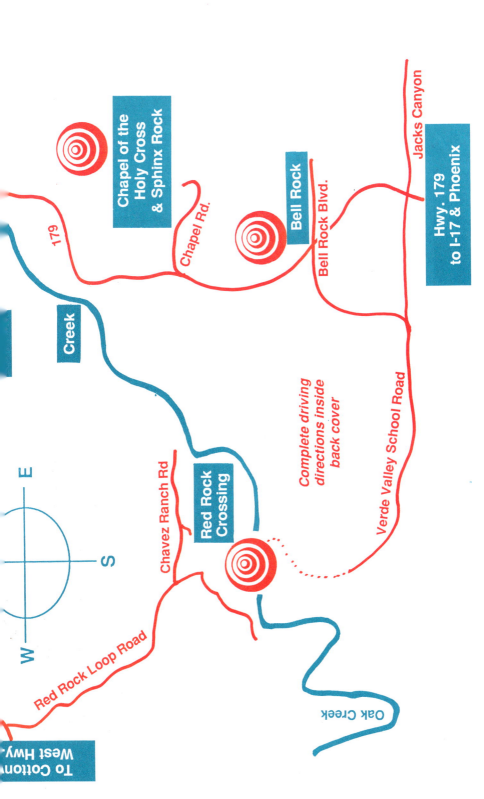

CENTERING AND GROUNDING

There are many ways of centering and grounding. Various methods are taught in the practice of yoga, meditation, centering. When one's heart is open without being aligned with a strong center of gravity, the person is a "pushover." I can literally push you over or push you off balance if your heart center is not aligned with your active power center or "Hara."

The "Hara" as it is called in Martial Arts, is your personal power center. Three inches below your navel, the Hara is the physical center of gravity in the body. Your Hara center is also the center of your universe. Once cognizant of this balance and power center, you can then become more aware of what "knocks" you off center and what assists you in maintaining balance.

CENTERING IN THE HARA Stand with feet about shoulder width apart. Let your knees be flexible - not locked back. Sway slightly to the left and right . Come to rest in the place where you are balanced over the fulcrum of each foot. Feel the way your weight is balanced over your feet. Then sway slightly back and forth and come to rest again in the most balanced place.

Breathe deeply and allow your mind to quiet itself, so that all idle chatter dissolves. Put your hand on your Hara and breathe into that area. On the inhale your body should expand like a balloon. On the exhale the body will "deflate." Feel the energy, power and life in your breath. Imagine energy spiraling in and out as you breathe. Work at spiraling the Hara in and out as you breathe.

GROUNDING Grounding is a simple yet profound exercise that connects us to the Earth. As you stand centered in your Hara power and energy, drop a silver cord from the tail of your spine deep into the core of the earth. Then let your feet become rooted in the earth like a mighty tree. Imagine that your strong, spiraling roots go deep into the Mother Earth. Your deep-rootedness will give you the flexibility to weather the storms of life while reaching your branches toward the light.

Page 12.

INTEGRATION

This powerful exercise integrates the energies of Mother Earth and Father Sky; the masculine/feminine polarities; Yin/Yang energies; God/Goddess, and all that is. The two merging triangles in the Star of David are symbolic of this integrative process.

In this exercise, let your hands and arms be soft and responsive to the energies of Mother Earth and Father Sky. The more you learn to respond to the energies, the deeper you will be able to experience them.

Center and ground yourself. As always, breathe deeply from your Hara. Then, with sensitive hands, bend the knees and dip down into the energy coming up from the Earth. Scoop the energy up into your hands, bring it up and through your body, into each of your Charkra centers. Raise the energy up above your head and offer it up to Father Sky. Let the Energy of Father Sky combine with the energy of Mother Earth and then shower down upon you and the Earth Mother. Dip down and scoop up the energies of Mother Earth again. Breathing deeply, bring the energies up, through your body and Chakra centers and offer them to Father Sky. Again, feel the energies merge and shower down upon you and the Earth Mother. Repeat this cycle 5 - 10 times; feel the energies intensify each time. Then, feel the integrated energies of Father/Mother God; the masculine/feminine; Yin/Yang, all flowing through you. Feel the love and gratitude from these integrated energies. Hold this energy in your heart center. Place your hands over your heart, integrating the polarities within your own body. Breathe deeply and let the melded energies flow out through your body and emanate as a healing force in your life, community, country, and planet. Enjoy the rich, peaceful feeling.

You may want to sing a mantra such as "The Earth is our Mother..." or "Blessings to the Sky Father..."

Like the developing stages of galaxies, we extend our center of energy and light out into the Universe through spiraling movements.

THE SPIRAL AS A UNIVERSAL VORTEX

The spiral is a symbol of growth, power, wisdom, creativity, eternity, and change. It is used to symbolize the orbit of the moon, to show the relationship between unity and multiplicity, to denote cosmic forms in motion and it is used as a schematic image of the evolution of the universe.

The spiral can be found in three main forms: a) <u>expanding</u> - like our solar system, other galaxies, and the universe itself; b) <u>contracting</u> - like whirlpools and whirlwinds; c) <u>ossified</u> - like the shell of a snail or conch. Since ancient times, a clockwise spiral represents creative power and a spiral with a counter-clockwise direction signifies destruction. In ancient cultures the spiral also symbolized the relationship of breath and spirit.

Spiral forms appeared frequently in the art of the Middle Ages. Spiral movements were thought to induce a state of ecstasy that enabled humankind to enter dimensions beyond the physical/ material world. By becoming aware of subtle spiraling energies, we can begin to truly dance ourselves into new dimensions.

THE SPIRALING DANCE OF LIFE

From the smallest particle of DNA in our cells to the largest galaxies in the universe, we can see the spiraling dance of life. The vortex energies of whirlpools and tornadoes move in a counter-clockwise spiral. Spirals of light energy move through the Chakras of our body in a clockwise direction. By imitating the positive, clockwise spiraling pattern we can open up our dormant energies and feel one with the universal dance of life.

New behaviors in both animals and humans are learned and mastered through imitation. We can imitate the spiraling dance of the universe with our body movements. We can imagine our breath, thoughts, emotions, and consciousness spiraling out into infinity to form an inseparable oneness with all that is. We can imagine spirals of energy rising out of the Earth Mother - blending, integrating, and becoming one with the energies spiraling down from Father Sky. The use, imitation, and imagination of spiraling energy in our body, mind, emotions, and spirit is a major key to mastery, manifestation, and creativity.

Here are a few exercises that will assist you in realigning your energies with the spiraling dance of the universe.

EGG BEATER   Let the arms hang from their sockets loose, limp and relaxed. With the back of the hand, *imitate* and then feel a clockwise spiral of energy. Move the hand in a circle - creating an egg-beater effect. Move the spiral of energy up through your hand to your wrist, elbow and upper arm. Then open up your shoulders with large circle movements. Your hands and forearms will cross and lift in front of your body much like the movement of a ballet dancer. Allow your armpits to open up, and receive some energy, air, and light. (We've been in the dark pits too long!) Follow your right hand with your eyes, then follow your left hand. Alternate your arm movements as if you are doing the backstroke in a swimming pool. Return to large circle movements, then small circles. Let the energy spiral back down the arms, elbows, wrists and hands. Return to the egg-beater motion with the back of the hands. Relax, and feel the energies that you have generated in your shoulders, arms and hands. As we learn to work with this vortex of spiraling energy, we can release stress and tension that have been held in the body. You can practice this exercise while you are sitting at your desk, in your car, or while sitting on "the throne."

HULA HOOP   Stand in a centered, balanced position, with your feet at least shoulder width apart. Imagine that your feet are like strong tree roots going deep into the earth. Begin to see, feel and *imagine* a spiral of energy, moving in a clockwise direction, coming up from the earth beneath your feet. Vividly imagine this spiraling vortex of energy. Breathe deeply, relax, and allow your feet and ankles to conform to the configuration of movement coming up through them. Keep your feet and ankles moving slowly to the spiraling vortex of energy that you are vividly imaging. Allow the movement and energy to come up slowly to your calves and then to your knees. (The movements are similar to those used with a hula hoop.) Breathe deeply at each major body part - ankles, calves, knees, thighs, hips, etc. - especially if you feel any held tension in those parts. The spiraling movements loosen old energy held in the body and the breath releases it. The breath is very important here.

Continue feeling and imagining the spiraling movement as you follow this movement with your thighs, hips, and abdomen. Breathe and release at each Chakra center. Allow the spiraling vortex of energy to move slowly up the trunk of your body, through your neck, and out the top of your head as you continue to breathe and release. When the vortex has passed completely through your body, become aware of the new feeling of expanded energy and oneness that you are experiencing.

BE LIKE A BIRD IN FLIGHT

Schnebly Hill and the Airport Vortex have large, safe, flat rock areas where you can begin to experience some of the laws of aerodynamics and levitation as you become "like a bird in flight." The following exercise can be a wonderful, exhilarating experience when practiced on a high hill, butte, or mesa. Wear a sleeveless top or bathing suit for this exercise so that so your entire arms are free to float and fly in a vortex of energy. Before you begin this exercise shake your hands and arms until they are loose and relaxed. Then center and ground yourself. Breathe deeply and through color, sound, or temperature, attune yourself to the energies around you. There are other energies all around, invisible yet real, thick like a cosmic soup.

Letting your arms dangle loosely from your sides, begin to gently stir the "cosmic soup" with your hands. Begin to play with the energies at your side. Allow your hands and arms to stir, circle, move, pulse, and flow in and out like the movements of a jellyfish. Soon you will begin to feel a vortex of energy around your hands and arms. They begin to almost float out from your sides. Allow the movement of your arms to build. Let the vortex of air lift and raise your arms until you feel the energy under your armpits. Continue the pulsating, floating movement until you are "flying like an eagle." You will begin to realize and feel the "thick cosmic soup" that birds fly through - much like our experience of swimming in water.

EXTEND INTO THE VAST MAGNIFICENCE OF YOUR BEING

Like a proud peacock opening its brilliant array of multicolored plumage, we can now extend our consciousness, experience our vastness, and embody our magnificence.

Until recently, we human beings could only experience our multicolored nature by leaving the body or by moving into an altered state that was very different from normal waking consciousness. Now, we know that a well-prepared mind/body can not only accept this expanded consciousness but can also operate out of this vastness much of the time.

We are vast, multi-dimensional, magnificent beings and our vastness reaches as deep within as it extends far outward. There are universes of inner space as well as wondrous galaxies in outer space to be discovered, explored, and understood. Because the visual sense is predominant for most people it is easier to explore outer worlds. So, let's explore!

You are as vast as your conscious awareness can extend. Look out onto the Red Rocks. You are that vast. Breathe deeply and extend your consciousness out to the rocks. Look to the horizon beyond the Red Rocks. You are that vast. While breathing deeply, extend your consciousness out to the horizon. Look up at the clouds floating in the great blue sky. You are that vast. Breathe deeply and extend your consciousness to one cloud, then another, and another. Then extend into the outer space of the blue sky and/or to the moon.

Why are we so awed when we look into the starry heavens on a clear night? Because we are that vast. On a clear night, pick a favorite star, planet, or constellation and extend your consciousness out to other galaxies and solar systems. Experience your vastness, then return your conscious awareness to your heart center. Feel your vastness there. Place your hands over your heart center, breathe deeply and anchor this new feeling of magnificence into your being.

You are vast. **Claim it! Be it!** There is truly nowhere to go and nothing to do for this expanded Self-concept. From the universes within to the universes without, you only have to accept that the greatness and the vastness is in fact, YOU - a Continuum of Divine Awareness.

The "technology" is here for us to open up to our Divine nature and to bring that Divinity into total waking consciousness. Then, we will live joyous, creative lives of love and peace as the Vast, Divine Beings that we are.

Be Vast! Be the vortex of energy that you are. **Spiral the energies of your Divine Self into your mind, body, beingness, and into the circumstances of your life.** You can be a vortex of abundance for yourself and everyone around you. You can be a vortex of health and vibrant energy for yourself and for everyone around you. You can be a vortex of love for yourself and everyone around you.

Choose it! Choose to experience and be a vast vortex of love, abundance, health, and peace for everyone around you.

Say each of the following affirmations three times - first, say the words mentally. Then say the affirmation with your mind and lips. Then make a strong, audible declaration and feel the resonance of Truth within your body.

I AM A VORTEX OF LOVE FOR MYSELF AND EVERYONE AROUND ME. (repeat 3 times)

I AM A VORTEX OF ABUNDANCE FOR MYSELF AND EVERYONE AROUND ME. (repeat 3 times)

I AM A VORTEX OF HEALTH AND VIBRANT ENERGY FOR MYSELF AND EVERYONE AROUND ME. (repeat 3 times)

IMAGES FROM THE PAST

Past-life images are often activated at Sedona's power points. A picture, feeling, or memory may easily surface. You will begin to feel that something not from the present moment is going on...

"*I walked down to the creek to take a cool swim. My bare feet seemed to mold themselves around the redrock flagstones, cobbles, and boulders. I was somewhat hunched over as I hopped from stone to stone. As the soles of my feet touched the cool stones, I felt a strong energy; then, as I looked down at my naked feet upon the rocks, I experienced a flashback of myself as an Indian walking upon these same stones.*

"While sitting in the Chapel of the Holy Cross, listening to the music there and meditating, an intense, whirling, spiraling energy seemed to come up from the floor. I felt and saw a strange time and culture. I was in an ancient temple filled with magnificent colored lights. Tears began to stream down by face.."

"My wife and I were hiking out past Sphinx rock. As we rounded the base of the first spire, to enter the canyon, we had to cross a small wash. I took Marie's hand to help her across the water. We both glanced down into the shallow pool. Blue and green colors from the sky and pines flashed into our eyes. We almost lost our balance and sat down. We saw and felt ourselves as a pair of dolphins swimming through these canyons and caverns. We both had the same experience!"

TUNING INTO THE DEJA VU

Your strongest physical sense will usually pick something up - a sound, color, feeling, smell. You can build on that sense and expand into the sound, color, feeling or smell by allowing your mind to believe that the experience is interesting, fun and/or worth exploring further. Many people let their conscious mind judge the experience as foolishness or "just my imagination." The memory then shuts off. Don't worry that it might be "just your imagination." Let it be a wonderful imaginary experience and exercise.

You have been given one piece of a past-life puzzle. Encourage your mind to fill in the missing pieces. Ask yourself these questions: Is it day or night? Warm or cold? Am I inside or outside? With other people or by myself? Are there any smells in the air or sounds in the background? Am I male or female? What kind of garments do I feel or see on my body? What am I doing? Is there anything in my hands or on my hands? Am I sitting, standing, sleeping or walking? Where am I going? Etc. etc. etc. Let your mind "play" with the images until you have a fairly good grasp of the

entire experience. Ask yourself what was the purpose of that lifetime. What were the lessons learned or not learned? Are there any incompletions to be resolved? If so, how? What areas need forgiveness? What can I give thanks for in that lifetime? How is that lifetime similar to my life now? How is it different? What kind of realizations can I make now?

Past life experiences can assist us in clearing core beliefs and old habit patterns that keep us in loss, lack, and separation. Use the experience of past life recall to forward your progress in this life, not to cram more data into your conscious mind data bank.

ⓒ TAKING THE MAGIC HOME

"I love the Red Rocks. I wish I could take some of this beauty back to Boston." "This is an incredible experience but what happens when we go back to our old routine jobs? Won't boredom, apathy and indifference return?" We frequently hear comments like these from many people who visit Sedona.

People either take photographs of their vacations or buy some kind of souvenir as a visual reminder of their fun and good times. Souvenirs get dusty; photos go into bottom drawers and memories and experiences fade. But, those good experiences don't have to fade away like some childhood sweetheart. We can call back the memories and re-create the same good feelings with a technique from Neuro-Linguistic Programming (NLP) called "anchoring."

Anchoring is merely a stimulus-response trigger mechanism. Most of the time we are unaware that some feeling, image or experience is being anchored into our consciousness. A song on the radio will bring up feelings about an old love. The smell of baked bread will call forth images from grandmother's kitchen.

You can call back any of the special Sedona Vortex Experiences that you have had and take your "vastness" home, by anchoring each experience into the physical body through touch, sound, smell and/or a strong visual image. In order to re-access the feeling or desired internal state at a later date, you simply call into awareness the strong visual image or smell, and repeat the sound and touch. (We do this all the time with our favorite foods.)

ANCHORING THE EXPERIENCE When you feel (even slightly) an exalted state like love, peace, oneness, etc. - anchor the feeling into your body/mind by placing your hands over your heart. Breathe deeply. Then find a sound that expresses your expanded feeling. Listen deeply and let the sound come to you. It may be the sound of the wind or the song of a bird. It can be a deep, low "OM" or a high-pitched whistle. Let the sound of your internal experience come forward, like crying when sad or laughing when happy. Make the sound audible and repeat it several times. Then, where- ever you go, you can re-create and re-experience your exalted state by putting your hands over your heart (the touch) while repeating the sound.

BECOME A VORTEX OF HEALING ENERGY FOR THE EARTH

Many people come to Sedona hoping for a life-changing vortex experience. We forget that <u>we</u> are a vortex of healing energy and that <u>we</u> can be a channel of energy to help heal and lift the Planet. "To give is to receive." As we give to the Earth Mother, we receive her many blessings. Oftentimes, we also forget to honor the Sacred lands that surround Sedona. The following outline has successfully served many Sedona residents and visitors in becoming a vortex of healing energy for the Planet. Expand or alter the outline according to your own guidance.

1. Find a spot that you resonate with or are called to.
2. Ask permission of the Guardian Spirits if you can enter the area and, if granted, walk in barefooted (if possible.)
3. After thoughtful prayer and meditation, state your intention for being there.
4. To prepare the body, mind and spirit for healing work do some stretching exercises and spiraling movements.
5. Center and ground your energies.
6. Surround yourself with the Light of the Christ. Invoke assistance from the Guardian Spirits, the Four Directions, and your Teachers, Guides and Masters.
7. Offer cornmeal, tobacco and/or prayers of Thanksgiving to the Spirit Helpers and to Mother Earth.
8. Begin to bring the energies up from Mother Earth through your physical body and Heart Center and offer them to Father Sky. Receive the energies from Father Sky, bring them through your physical body and Heart Center, and gently place them in the Earth Mother. Continue this cycle of integration until you feel a sense of completion, peace and/or wholeness.
9. Tune into any Deja Vu awareness that is coming up.
10. Release any blocked energies in the earth or yourself, due misunderstandings or a lack of forgiveness.
11. Allow even more healing energies to flow to you by breathing like the wind.
12. Expand into vastness.
13. Extend the vastness and healing energies to some particular place or group of people.
14. Have a time of silent meditation, then anchor the feeling in your heart.
15. Leave in love and gratitude.
16. Take the expanded experience of yourself as a vortex of healing energy home and quietly share it with your special part of Planet Earth.